THESE WOMEN YOU GAVE ME

Also by Antoinette Brim

Icarus in Love
Psalm of the Sunflower

THESE WOMEN
YOU GAVE ME

Antoinette Brim

Indolent Books

Cover art: *BWR (black, white, red) naked #04* by Frédéric Glorieux
licensed under CC BY-SA 2.0

Book design: Nieves Guerra

Published by Indolent Books,
an imprint of Indolent Arts Foundation, Inc.

www.indolentbooks.com
Brooklyn, New York
ISBN: 978-1-9450-2305-7

CONTENTS

for Demetrice Anntía Worley

DELICATE RUIN: LILITH'S LAMENT

He said, "It is not good for man to be alone." He then created a woman for Adam, from the earth, as He had created Adam himself, and called her Lilith. Adam and Lilith began to fight. She said, "I'll not lie below," and he said, "I will not lie beneath you, but only on top. For you are fit only to be in the bottom position, while I am to be in the superior one." Lilith responded, "We are equal to each other inasmuch as we were both created from the earth." But they would not listen to one another. When Lilith saw this, she pronounced the Ineffable Name and flew away into the air. Adam stood in prayer before his Creator: "Sovereign of the universe!" he said, "The woman you gave me has run away."

—The *Alphabet of Ben Sira*

Lilith to Adam

I.

stardust/clay/morning dew   we both were
thrown/spun about the Potter's Wheel/we both were
given   fowl/beast/leviathan   dominion

Together, we could lie beneath
a new moon   or   the south wind

Adam, writhe with me in blue-black shadows
          submit to me   and I will   submit to you.

II.

Another?

there can be no other—
as full as the moon
who pulls the tides at will—

Alas,

we both were,   but now Eve is:
not thigh bone   nor skull
but splintered rib.

Lilith to Eve

I.

Rib of his rib   bone of his bone
mother of all living   stain

Adam forsaken
Satan beguiled
Cain/Abel/Seth   split you wide

Will they name your daughters:
          That woman You gave me?

II.

Since I would not lie beneath Adam;
Since I rode the wind   [His Name reined in my hand]—

I must gather spilled seed
to bare ghosts   who will die.

Lilith and Eve: we are sisters
failed wives

whose children
fall   daily.

Lilith swears to spare Adam's seed

According to legend, Lilith promised to spare Adam's children
if the names of three angels, Sanvi, Sansanvi and Semangelaf,
were written near them.

A baby's breath with its chalky sweet, milk-silk air
can conjure mother love into charcoaled circles to bar me.

Sanvi, Sansanvi and Semangelaf

But, a baby's breath—for all its sweetness, hosts a sour note—
white buds atop its tongue will bloom into rebellion.

Sanvi, Sansanvi and Semangelaf

The Afflatus imparts Will. Lungs fill with Autonomy.
Spare your own heart. Snatch its breath yourself.

Lilith laments her lost children

It is futile to take aim and piss against a wall.
A yellow stain is more man than one who whines

to God. I've bled a sea of knotted rusted blooms:
an exodus of sloughed womb and dropped fruit.

I've borne down, birthing clots and stones,
to whom I cannot offer my breast.

Each new moon voids me; pulls life from me.
I have bled out sons and daughters

into snow and sand; mountain and valley. I have bled,
until all tributaries have flown back into me, their source.

Lilith petitions God

I did not lay
the serpent's egg.
I did not hatch forth
from it. You created
its delicate shell—inlaid
jewel and alabaster;

When You created Lucifer,
his vocal chords silver
sinew and measured pitch;
his person encrusted with
gems and light; this loving
excess was his eggshell.

Your joy at his being was
the yolk that fed his pride;
Until that pride swelled and
cracked open his ordained place,
causing You to fling him from heaven.

Lucifer surfaced in Paradise—
full grown, self-seeking.
Shards of his serpent shell
pierced Eve's foot
[when she walked through the Garden
admiring the sovereign tree].
Poison traveled to her heart
compelling her to eat; and Adam with her

fell; and with them all of mankind
fell and all of creation fell
into a plan of redemption.

I am Lilith.
Your firstborn daughter.
must I continue to fall
without hope of
redemption?

Lilith taunts the righteous

You, submitted sovereigns: black day   lit night—
lie in Abraham's bosom   far from Edom   far from Eden
scratch seed furrows in dust, and eat the grit that bore us.

Await   the consuming fire   the everlasting flame—
perch fast on rocks   stop your ears   clench shut your eyes
against your brethren   in travail.

Sharon is like the steppe. Bashan and Carmel are stripped bare.
Wildcats and hyenas circle about the remnant.
Bask in the terror.

You, submitted sovereigns:
will trudge through your brethren's blood.
Goat-demons shall call to each other;   there too,

I, Lilith   shall repose and find a place to rest.

In her image

Rab Judah citing Samuel ruled: If an abortion had the likeness of Lilith its mother is unclean by reason of the birth, for it is a child but it has wings.
—Babylonian Talmud, Tractate Niddah 24b

The night is a lonely house. Without roof or floor,
I make water like a beast, with only my hair to cover me.
Raven-tressed and winged, I wear the moon
around my neck as a jewel. My eyes are clear as coal
before time and burden presses it into nakedness.

Women lower their eyes at my spoken name:
Lilith. Queen of Adam. Hag. Sovereign. Free.

And, when they are raped in the night, by husband
or friend or fiend, their thighs pressed into splotches
of amethyst and lapis pools under thin skin, their
bruised fruit (cursed and teased out of them),
is in my image: winged, angry and intent upon flight.

Lilith muses aloud

A woman can:

be the mother of all,
the mother of God
or the woman who hung the scarlet thread

be the woman who gleaned,
the woman who judged
or the woman whose hair washed His feet

be the first at the tomb,
carry a portent in her womb
or be labored for—for fourteen years

or a woman can:

hide in the hollow of trees; part
raptor; part temptress; all legend
and lie; singing into the night chill
a tortured trill of regret; alone
and unable to die.

Lilith dreams

Amidst the waters of the firmament:

male and female float; as only indigo shadows
stitched to the depths with light can do;

the underside of a knee presses
the small of a back;

the waters resist, then
break away into current and lift;

her inky plumed crown
floats above her, clothes her

tangles about him,
enshrouds them, while

a moonless sky leaves the night
undisturbed; complacent.   Complicit.

Lilith lost in *tlun*
(or snow that sparkles in the moonlight)

In this fallen world, there is constant snow;

ylaipi folds into *nylaipin* on our children's tongues.

We become snow angels under *mortla*;

our children will bury us in the storm we (ourselves) have conjured.

Lilith knows this. She has read the Book and found her name erased.

We will all be *naklin.*

***

In this fallen world, there is constant snow;

tomorrow's snow folds into the snows of yesteryear on our children's
                                                              tongues.

We will become snow angels under the mounds of the dead;

our children will bury us in the storm we (ourselves) have conjured.

Lilith knows this. She has read the Book and found her name erased.

We will all become forgotten snow.

Lilith meditates on the blue sound

never seen   so many   shades of blue
each wrestling   for a scrap of sky:
lapis lazuli stone   against crackled

water relenting   mottled blue fall
into the sound: constant fugue-like counterpoint;
steel-blue crinoline   floating above   frothy lace

somewhere in the world   black sky meets black ocean;   he
huddles secure   warmed by fire   awaiting first light
when the blues will leave me   to delight him

Lilith away

After Henry Dumas

I am cold
wings flying

I am in you—
you are without

we were

now,
the sun in black
sighs

EDEN'S INTERLUDE: CLAY & BONE

Watch Woman

He fashioned them both. First Adam. Then Lilith. Both. Fashioned from the peat of my heart. I loved them. Both. Adam awoke with furrowed brow. Lilith with a gasp followed by a sigh. They sprung full-grown into me.

But Lilith did not see herself through Adam's eyes.

Lilith bent over the still water and saw Lilith. Dark eyes. Black roping hair falling forward. She knew herself to be a recipe of mud and clay, morning dew and stardust. Of raven luft and oxen shoulder. I knew she would not lie beneath.

I tell you this because Lilith is more than discarded and profane. I loved her. I love her. Still.

I met Eve at twilight. The moon nudged its way into the horizon to peek at her. The four winds stopped, and turned to watch the Afflatus animate thin bone. She opened her eyes to Adam leaning over her. His broad body almost blocked out all of Eden. Adam sought to fill her eyes. His sage and sand scent filled her nostrils. His heavy breath filled her ears. She awakened beneath.

THAT WOMAN YOU GAVE ME:
EVE EXPLAINS

Eve/ Woman/ Wife

The LORD God said, "It is not good for the man to be alone.
I will make a helper suitable for him."
—*Genesis 2:18*

Breath in my face quickens me—
to light   sky   eager eyes

He calls me Eve/ Woman/ Wife
I have no language for him.

I am so new/weak. Enthralled
by Eden: locus of life—

Pools of lapis lazuli,
blue as the four rivers' source.

Her forests of ebony;
streams of iridescent koi.

Birds of Paradise take wing
call from low branches to me—

teach me "home."   Rock-roses release
blooms to settle in my hair.

Eden loves me. And I, her.
But he calls himself Adam.

He calls me Eve/ Woman/ Wife.
face to face; he takes my hand—

palm to palm, our hands rest still:
mine is lithe;   his is thick, strong—

he pulls me, the space between
us escapes. He is sandalwood and musk.

His head and chin are lamb's wool
His voice is quiet thunder.

Eden's breeze musses my hair.
Adam's hand brushes it back.

I leave Eden; fold into
Adam. Know woman/wife—

Lie beneath. Yield. Mouth to mouth.
The earth rises to meet me.

I fall open, and   apart,
pressed beneath Adam and Earth,

I discover myself through
his touch: The bend of my legs;

the arch of my back; fullness
of breast, belly and voice.   Eve.

EDEN'S INTERLUDE: FREE FALL

Free Fall

In the beginning, we knew only bliss. There was no rain, just a gentle rolling mist captured beneath heaven's firmament and the earth. Giddy, I received Adam and Lilith to my breast. And it was good. Until Lilith pronounced the Ineffable Name and flew away.

Shortly thereafter, the music in Heaven was muted by war. The Morning Star had gone dark, judged himself too lowly exalted and sought the throne of God. Even so, war was little more than a light show for all of Eden. Just pinkish hues exploding into chrysanthemum bursts. Lilith watched from the highest limbs of the Tree of Life. Already fallen, she had not been beguiled.

But Eve did not know Lucifer. Did not know Pride. Did not know Death. Did not know. And the fruit in his hand was beautiful to eat and why wouldn't she want to be like God? What is good, when all about you is good? What is evil, when all about you is good? What is death, when all about you lives forever? And Lucifer, his vocal chords, still silver sinew and elegant whine. His person still jewel encrusted, still standing on two muscled legs was so beguiling. But Eve did not know beguiling, did not know deceive, and did not know spite. She could not have known.

The Host peered over the edge of Heaven. Gabriel exhaled a slow, shallow breath. Michael unsheathed his sword. The Seraphim assembled. But, God raised his hand to let Eve be.

And she took of its fruit and ate, and she also gave some to her husband who was with her, and he ate.

Eden Away

I, Eden,

am raptured into Heaven

emptied of Adam/Eve/Lilith.

                                    Empty.

REMNANT & RUIN: EVE'S LAMENT

Knowing

And the LORD God said, "The man has now
become like one of us, knowing good and evil."
—*Genesis 3:22*

I have plucked the stars from their
swaddling board. Set the moon

on her wane. Taught the lion
to eat the lamb. Learned to lie.

I crush blossoms in my fists.
Regret all broken tethers.

Adam is cold. I am cold.
The fire is not enough.

Our heads are full of what we
did not know before the fruit:

Chisel branches to spears. Need
excuses murder. Once friend,

now food. Now blanket. Now warmth.
It matters little, what is

good or evil. Adam is
warm. Adam is fed. Adam.

Adam is angry, blames me;
says, "that woman you gave me."

But, my seed will bruise Satan's
head; restore heaven and earth.

When my womb brings redemption,
Adam will forgive all this.

I am bloodied—no longer
beautiful. I am broken.

Bramble and thistle crown my
matted hair. With wind-burned face,

gouged knees, sunken eyes,   I am
no longer Eden's Eve—but

I am Adam's mate, and the
only like him. Without his God

to walk with him in the cool
of evening, I can give warmth.

To him, I offer my hand
now rough and torn. He accepts.

His hand crushes mine, pulls me/
drags me. I do not wince.

Pain is no longer new. This
is not Eden. My back rests

on stones that rock and resist.
Our breath bursts into clouds

and then dissipates. The moon
hides her face, as I tear, bleed.

I do not wince. His grip dams
the blood from my hands. Rivers

of spittle converge like the
headwaters that mist Eden—

Come to me   in the midst with
dew for my parched tongue. Blossoms

for my hair. Aloe for my wounds.
Forgive. My naiveté

has doomed Creation.   Unless
Adam's seed takes root in me.

NOTES

The excerpt from the Alphabet of Ben Sira is translated by Norman Bronznick in *Rabbinic Fantasies: Imaginative Narratives from Classical Hebrew Literature* (Yale Judaica Series), edited by David Stern and Mark Jay Mirsky. Jewish Publication Society (1990).

Lilith lost in *tlun* (or snow that sparkles in the moonlight). These are Inuit words for snow from *The Eskimos' Hundred Words for Snow* by Phil James: **tlun**, snow sparkling with moonlight; **ylaipi**, tomorrow's snow; **nylaipin**, the snows of yesteryear; **mortla**, snow mounded on dead bodies; **naklin**, forgotten snow.

Lilith taunts the righteous echoes verses from the *Isaiah*, Chapters 33-34.

Free Fall. The final line quotes Genesis 3:6.

In her image. The excerpt from the Babylonian Talmud is as quoted by Judith R. Baskin in Midrashic Women: Formations of the Feminine in Rabbinic Literature. Brandeis University Press (2015).

Eve/ Woman/ Wife. The epigraph is from the New International Version of the Bible.

Knowing. The epigraph is from the New International Version of the Bible.

ACKNOWLEDGMENT

"Lilith Muses Aloud" appeared in *Radius: Poetry from the Center to the Edge.*

ABOUT THE AUTHOR

Antoinette Brim is the author of *Icarus in Love* (Main Street Rag, 2013) and *Psalm of the Sunflower* (Aquarius Press/Willow Books, 2010). She is a Cave Canem Foundation fellow, a recipient of the Walker Foundation Scholarship to the Fine Arts Work Center in Provincetown, and a Pushcart Prize nominee. Her work has appeared in numerous journals and magazines as well as in the anthologies *Villanelles* (in the Everyman's Library Pocket Poets series; Everyman's Library, 2012), edited by Annie Finch and Marie-Elizabeth Mali; *Stand Our Ground: Poems for Trayvon Martin and Marissa Alexander* (FreedomSeed Press, 2013), edited by Ewuare X. Osayande; *Critical Insights: Alice Walker* (Salem Press, 2012), edited by Nagueyalti Warren; *44 on 44: Forty-Four African American Writers on the 44th President of the United States* (Third World Press, 2011), edited by Lita Hooper, Sonia Sanchez, and Michael Simanga; *Not A Muse: The Inner Lives of Women* (Haven Books, 2010), edited by Jennifer Karmin and Vivien Jones; *Just Like A Girl: A Manifesta!* (GirlChild Press, 2008), edited by Michelle Sewell; and *The Whiskey of our Discontent: Gwendolyn Brooks as Conscience and Change Agent* (Haymarket Books, 2017), edited by Quraysh Ali Lansana and Georgia A. Popoff. Brim serves as the President of the Board of the Creative Arts Workshop in New Haven, Conn., and is an Assistant Professor of English at Capital Community College in Hartford, Conn.

Photo credit: Katrina Goldburn

ABOUT INDOLENT BOOKS

Indolent Books is a small independent poetry press founded in 2015 and operating in Brooklyn. Indolent champions innovative, provocative, risky poems and the poets who write them, especially voices from underrepresented communities.

www.ingramcontent.com/pod-product-compliance
Lightning Source LLC
Chambersburg PA
CBHW052056160425
25224CB00041B/326